Dad Gone

Eris Aubrie Busey

Tellwell Talent
www.tellwell.ca

ISBN
978-0-2288-3378-9 (Hardcover)
978-0-2288-3377-2 (Paperback)

Dedication

I would like to thank my Mother and Grandmother for helping me create the vision for my very first book.

Thank you to my big sister Niah for inspiring me; and my little brother Christian for being my reason to keep pushing.

A special thank you to my Great Grandmother "O.G." for her words of encouragement, I Love You!

I'm a straight "A" student, thanks Mom!

I hoped that you would surprise me for Career Day, but you didn't show up.

There was a front row seat reserved for
you at my fashion show that remained empty....

I really wanted you to join me at the Daddy Daughter Dance but you never came.

Daddy Daughter Dance

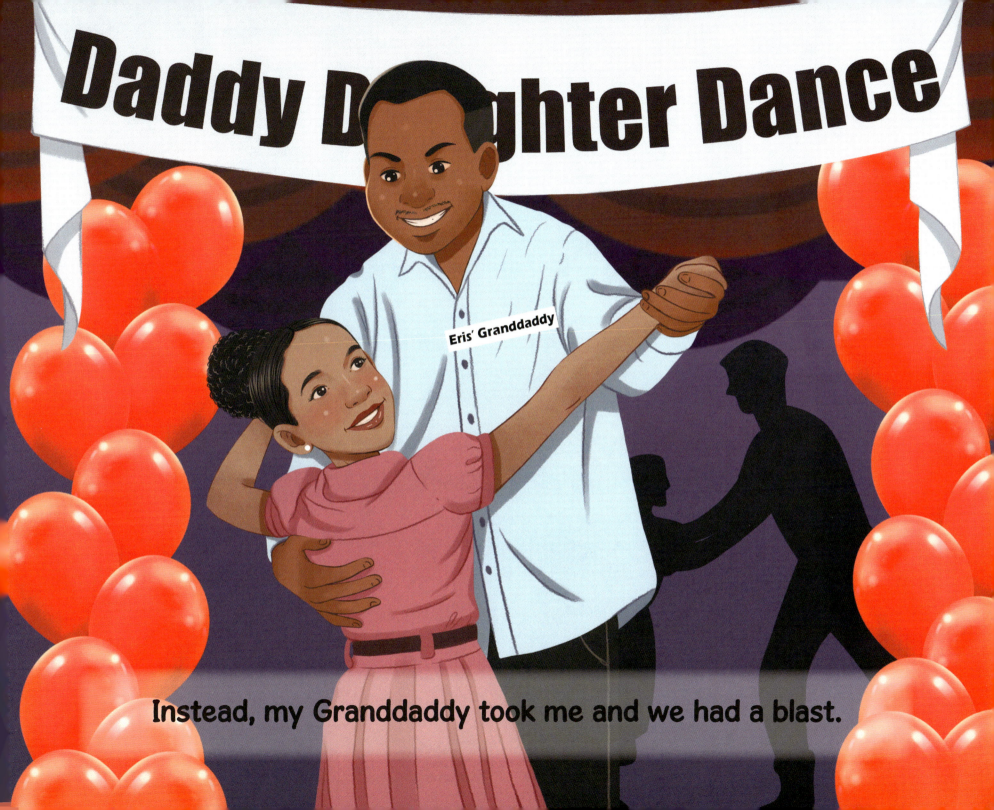

Daddy Daughter Dance

Eris' Granddaddy

Instead, my Granddaddy took me and we had a blast.

GRADUATION DAY

I graduated at the top of my fifth grade class.

Eris' Dad

You never showed up but the ones that love me did.

Without your applause,
your hugs or your kisses.

Without your Daddy Daughter
time and good well wishes.

I celebrate me and my
accomplishments with a Dad Gone.

CPSIA information can be obtained at www.ICGtesting.com
Printed in the USA
LVIW012216090221
678887LV00005B/144